WILDFLOWERS

of the

Mount Wilson Trails
and
San Gabriel Mountains

Text and Photographs
George Liskow

WILDFLOWERS

of the

Mount Wilson Trails
and San Gabriel Mountains
Southern California

ISBN Number 0-9628024-0-9

Color and Printing by WCP Colorgraphics

Front Cover

My good friends Dave Boyd from Indiana and Carlton Norris from Georgia on an early morning spring wildflower hike near Chantry Flats. The yellow wildflower in the upper left corner is Spanish broom, a flower introduced years ago from Europe.   So the cover shows three of my favorite non-natives, Dave, Carlton and Spanish broom.

Back Cover

A magnificent Our Lord's Candle elegantly standing watch on an early May morning looking down into the San Gabriel Valley.

Dedication

For my best friend, Ginny, to whom I'm lucky enough to be married.

Acknowledgements

My thanks to Ginny, without whose encouragement I should never have finished the manuscript. A number of her pictures have improved the photography section as well.

And to my friends Dave Boyd and Carlton Norris (on the cover) for their support, camaraderie and terrible shaggy dog stories.

The Los Angeles County Arboretum staff were not only gracious in giving their time, they were great fun to work with, and cheerfully provided answers to my endless questions. I had the benefit of a great body of knowledge in the persons of Suzanne Granger, Daryl Koutnik, Rosetta Bentley and Allen Howard, for each of whose contributions and encouragement I'm truly grateful. They have done much to improve the accuracy and specificity of the text, not to mention the spelling. (My Latin is terrible.)

I am also indebted to Melanie Baer of the Theodore Payne Foundation for her knowledgeable assistance and many helpful suggestions. Indeed, the Payne Foundation staff and volunteers were all of great assistance, and I appreciate the advice of Dennis Bryson, Therese Thompson and Ed Peterson.

Table of Contents

INTRODUCTION

I put this handbook together so that hikers and flower lovers might better enjoy some of the most exceptional yet often overlooked beauty of the wildflowers to be found on these trails. My idea was to give hikers a pictorial catalog, something to carry with them on the trail to show some of the flowers they are likely to see on the Mount Wilson trails or in the San Gabriel mountains generally; and to supply a little information about and identification of those flowers.

Incidentally, this is a book for enthusiasts, not botanists. Purists will probably be appalled by my informality. Some of my botanist friends have indeed raised their eyebrows at the non native flowers pictured, for instance. The exotics pictured are there because they're on the trails, and I suspect most readers won't care a lot whether they are intruders or natives. Indeed, many of the introduced flowers are among the prettier ones. If you want to clothe them in an air of mystery refer to them as "exotics", another name for non-native or introduced flowers.

As to the flowers in general, almost any time of year all one has to do is to look along the side of the trail to see a profusion of flowers of many sizes, colors and shapes; most of them beautiful, some of them odd, a few downright ugly, but all of them interesting. One remarkable characteristic of these flora is that they so tenaciously cling to life in such a terribly inhospitable environment and yet produce such beauty. There's a lesson in that somewhere. "Sweet are the uses of adversity..." (As You Like It; Act 2, Scene 1.)

I hope wild flower enthusiasts will find some new information of interest to them; I've included most of the scientific as well as the generally accepted common names their botanical families, something about their origin, uses and even menace where they pose any. I have also noted places on the trails where the flowers are likely to be found.

The pictures are arranged to make identification easy. The divisions follow the usage in the Audubon Society Field Guide to American Wildflowers.

The photographs are grouped first by color. Whites are followed by yellow/orange, then red, pink/purple and finally, blue. Within each color the flowers are ordered according to their shape: simple flowers, such as four and five petalled flowers; followed by daisy shaped; odd shaped, such as pea flowers and tubes; rounded clusters and last, elongated clusters. Strictly speaking, shapes and clusters are not the same thing, but this classification was devised for ease of identification, not precise scientific organization.

After the pictures come descriptions of each flower. The information is in alphabetical order by plant family name and within each family group by common name, also alphabetically.

The pictures and the descriptions are cross referenced to each other. That is, each text refers to the page where the flower is pictured; and each picture refers to the descriptive text.

When you find a flower on the trail you wish to identify, look first in the picture section for flowers of the same color. Note the shape of the flower (simple, daisy, odd, etc.) to locate that flower within the color. If it is included, then you will find a description on the page noted under the photograph.

The final section describes four of the six major trails to the top of Mount Wilson noting the flowers likely to be found on each. For the less energetic wildflower lovers I have also described several roads to Mount Wilson and into the San Gabriel Mountains where wildflowers may be found merely by driving one's car up the hill and keeping a sharp eye out.

The catalog does not purport to be complete by any means. Actually there are several hundred species of flowering plants in these mountains, but only eighty plus are pictured. Those shown are simply the ones I've found over a period of several years and are the most likely flowers a hiker will find. If you do locate one (or more) that I've missed, please let me know so I can add it to the next edition.

As to the names, I've used common names wherever possible and scientific names where there is no common name or I couldn't identify a common name. You will also find (latin) botanical species names of most of the flowers. They are a starting point for finding more information about the plants in question, because most botanical texts are keyed to latin species names. Except, of course, watch out for a couple of names I obviously made up.

I hope this manual will increase the readers' pleasure as well as their knowledge of these flowers. Enjoy!

George Liskow
Sierra Madre, California

PHOTOGRAPHS

1 *Prickly poppy* *p 69*

2 *Crimson spot rock rose* *p 71*

3 Morning glory   *p 58*

4 Blackberry   *p 72*

5 Rattlesnake weed   *p 74*

6 Woodland star   *p 73*

7 Miner's lettuce   *p 70*

8 Wild cucumber   *p 54*

9 Virgin's bower   *p 46*

10 Virgin's bower   *p 46*

11 Chickweed   *p 68*

12 Honesty   *p 59*

13 White nightshade   *p 61*

14 Cliff Aster   *p 77*

15 Wild sweet pea p 65

16 Black sage
p 56

17 Muilla maritima p 42

18 Eupatory   *p 79*

19 California everlasting   *p 77*

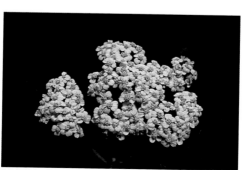

20 White Yarrow   *p 81*

21 Yerba santa   *p 84*

22 Sweet alyssum   *p 59*

23 Sugarbush   *p 76*

24 Yucca (Our Lord's candle) p 41

25 Ceanothus p 43

26 Chamise p 72

27 Chamise   *p 72*

28 Blazing star   *p 75*

29 Blazing star   *p 75*

30 Sun Cups   *p 49*

31 Hooker's evening   *p 48*
primrose

32 Hooker's evening primrose   *p 48*

33 Phil's evening primrose   *p 49*

34 Tree poppy   *p 70*

35 California poppy   *p 69*

36 California poppy   p 69

37 Cassia senna   page 63

38 Oxalis   p 61

39 Common sunflower   *p 78*

40 Senecio   *p 80*

41 Dandelion   *p 78*

2 and 43 Spanish broom (and other exotics) p 65

4 Yellow monkey flower p 52

21

45 Bush monkey flower   *p 50*

46 Tree tobacco   *p 61*

47 Large flowered lotus   *p 64*

48 Lotus
p 64

9 Deer vetch   *p 62*

50 and 51 Golden Yarrow *p 79*

52 Black mustard *p 58*

24

53 and 54 Western wallflower   *p 60*

55 Dodder   *p 57*

56 Indian pink   *p 68*

57 California fuschia   *p 47*

58 Scarlet monkey flower   *p 51*

59 Crimson columbine p 45

60 Keckiella (bush penstemon)
p 51

61 Indian paintbrush p 51

62 Scarlet larkspur p 46

63 Toyon (berry)   *p 73*

64 Prickly phlox   *p 67*

65 Crane's bill   *p 54*

66 Farewell to spring   p 48

67 Gilia   p 67

68 Mountain four-o'clock   p 53

69 Rock rose   *p 71*

70 Plummer's mariposa lily   *p 55*

71 Purple nightshade   *p 60*

72 Twiggy wreath plant *p 81*

73 Thistle *p 80*

74 Cal. Thistle *p 77*

31

75 Leafy daisy p 80

76 Elegant clarkia p 47

77 Parry's phacelia　　　　　　　　　　　*p 83*

78 Blue dicks　　　　　　　　　　　*p 42*

79 Psoralea　　　　　　　　　　　*p 64*

80 Chia   *p 57*

81 Cal. buckwheat   *p 44*

82 Stinging lupine   *p 65*

83 Jupiter's beard   *p 82*

84 Larkspur p 45

85 Bush lupine p 62

86 Caterpillar phacelia p 83

87 Eriastrum (phlox) p 66

88 Parry's turricula p 83

89 Showy penstemon p 52

90 Showy penstemon   p 52

91 Grinnell's penstemon   p 50

92 & 93 Baby blue eyes

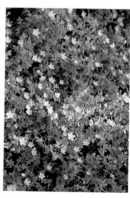

p 82

94 Ceanothus   *p 43*

95 Ceanothus   *p 43*

96 Fern—between First Water and Orchard Camp polypodium

7 Blue larkspur   p 44

98 Sierra Madre trail

9 Chantry Flat from Upper
Winter Creek

100 My friend, Bill, peering at a
madrone tree.

FLOWER DESCRIPTIONS

AGAVE FAMILY
Agavaceae

This family of almost 20 genera and 500 species has only one representative in the vicinity of Mount Wilson, the Yucca whipplei. These are really desert plants, and the one species here is found on the mountain sides mostly at lower levels.

Our Lord's candle   Pl. 24   *Yucca whipplei*

The plant looks like a big green hedgehog hugging the ground. Its leaves are long, slender and spiky with very sharp points a flower stalk as much as 12 feet tall. The tap root is almost endlessly deep. The creamy white flowers grow in quite large, elongated clusters, the flowers averaging about 1 1/2 inches in diameter, with clusters as much as 6 feet long and a foot or more in diameter.
This yucca is usually found on the open dry hillsides from sea level to about 3500 feet, blooming from April until June. Most years a real display may be seen all over the hillside on the lower parts of the Sierra Madre trail, looking indeed like huge white candles. Both the cover picture and plate 24 are of the same plant which was one of the largest of these I've seen. These yucca also virtually cover the hillsides in several stretches of the Angeles Crest Highway and Highway 39. After blooming season, the stalks dry up and the seed pods hanging from them look like so many small brown castanets.

AMARYLLIS FAMILY
Amaryllidaceae

This worldwide family embraces a large number of species. The family is closely related to the Lily family, and have some similar characteristics. They grow from bulbs, rhizomes or underground stems; the flowers characteristically appear in clusters at the end of long, leafless stalks. There are a number of cultivated amaryllis plants to be found in Southern California gardens.

Blue dicks   Pl. 78   *Dichelostemma pulchella*

The plant bearing these flowers is almost unnoticeable, growing as it does in mostly grassy areas. The leaves are long and slender, growing out of the base; they tend to melt into the grasses by which they are often surrounded. The light purple flowers are an inch or two across, and bloom at the end of a long leafless stem. You will find blue dicks in grassy areas on open parts of the trail, blooming from March to May. Usually several plants will be found growing close together. When you see one cluster of flowers you will usually find that it is growing in a small colony of plants. They are sometimes to be found on the downhill side of the Sierra Madre Trail; also on the Toll Road along open grassy areas.

Muilla   Pl. 17   *Muilla maritima*

This member of the amaryllis family is comparatively rare on the trails. When found, muilla will be in shady places. The flat clusters of small white flowers bloom April to June. The picture here was taken at First Water which is the kind of environment where this plant will typically be found.

BUCKTHORN FAMILY
Rhamnaceae

These evergreen shrubs or trees are found many places on the chaparral stretches of the trails. The plants grow as much as 18 feet high, with tiny flowers in elongated, sometimes foot long clusters at the end of their branches. An impressive stand of deep blue flowered shrubs may be seen south of the 210 freeway west of Montrose. In April the whole hillside seems to turn blue from the blooms.

Ceanothus   Pl. 25   *Ceanothus leucodermis*

Six to twelve feet tall, this evergreen shrub has pale green bark, spiny branches, and mostly white sometimes shading to very light blue flowers in clusters on the branch ends. Fairly rare, and only occasionally found along the Mount Wilson trails in the chaparral. *Leucodermis* blooms later than greenbark, generally April to June.

Greenbark ceanothus   Pl. 94, 95   *Ceanothus spinosus*

Greenbark ceanothus gets big - up to eighteen feet - and has smooth green bark on spiny branches. Flowers grow in long clusters like big blue popsicles. The tiny stamens are yellow; so that the flower clusters look blue from a distance, the yellow only becoming noticeable upon close inspection. Many plants can be found on the Toll Road and the lower parts of Sierra Madre; a few may be seen on Upper Winter Creek. Blooming begins in February and continues through May, somewhat depending upon altitude. Greenbark is obviously related to the ceanothus described above but clearly different in color.

BUCKWHEAT FAMILY
Polygonaceae

Only one member of this family is represented in this handbook, but there are several species in this area which can be found virtually everywhere. The species pictured is California buckwheat (*Eriogonum fasciculatum*), a small two to three foot shrub with dense balls of tiny pinkish flowers atop stiff erect stems. Buckwheat grows abundantly along all the trails and approach roads except Sturtevant Falls and Lower Winter Creek, and blooms from April to October. Bees make a fine honey from buckwheat and may almost always be heard buzzing among the flowers - so take care. Plate 81.

BUTTERCUP FAMILY
Ranunculaceae

The buttercup family embraces over 2000 species of mostly herbaceous plants and some vines, usually found in the cooler regions of North America. The flowers have many stamens and pistils, and the sepals and petals are often look pretty much alike.

Blue larkspur   Pl. 97   *Delphinium parryi*

An erect perennial herb to two or more feet high, blue larkspur is found in grassy places along the trails, mostly in shade or semi shade. Frequently found in shady spots along Lower Winter Creek; also in trailside niches, usually on the uphill side of Sierra Madre and Upper Winter Creek. The flowers are light blue; you may find the deep lavender larkspur in the same area. The flowers grow about two inches apart along the erect, somewhat scraggly stems and bloom during April and May.

Crimson columbine   Pl. 59   *Aquilegia formosa*

Striking red and yellow flowers about an inch across that remind me of a medieval jester's cap hang from the long curved stems of this plant. The flowers have red sepals with knobbed points on the back and yellow spreading petals. The yellow stamens and styles hang downward from the center. They bloom May to August. The plant likes moist spots in semi shade. Actually the only place I've found this beauty is near a small stream well up Highway 39; you might also look for columbine at First Water, on Lower Winter Creek or Sturtevant Falls. The Forest Service has sometimes planted columbine next to the information building at Crystal Lake campground. Formosa is derived from a Latin word for beautiful, quite an appropriate description of this flower.

Larkspur   Pl. 84   *Delphinium patens*

A spindly plant with only a few leaves, bearing violet flowers along the main stem. Less frequently encountered than blue larkspur, the stems grows to about sixteen inches in protected areas along the chaparral section of the Sierra Madre trail, on the uphill side where you find a little shade.

Scarlet larkspur Pl. 62 *Delphinium cardinale*

A tall conspicuous plant which blooms from May to July.
The flowers are brilliant red and quite noticeable from a
distance. Both the sepals and lower petals are red, the
upper petals yellow. The plants are found in the chaparral
environment. This is another flower I've seen only on
Highway 39. They grow along the road a mile or so above
the East Fork turn off, as well as near the dam on the
lower section of the road.

Virgin's bower Pl. 9, 20 *Clematis ligusticifolia*

A vine which gets 30 feet long, virgin's bower can virtually
covers small trees. The flowers have no petals, but four or
five petal like sepals. Stamens are abundant, and the
pistils grow long and silky, forming many greenish white
puff balls from April to June. The two plates show
different stages of the flower's development, the first
picture being the flower first in bloom, the second when it
has gone to seed. There is quite a difference. Virgin's
bower is relatively common; I've seen it near the top of
Mount Wilson on the Sturtevant Falls trail, on Upper
Winter Creek and on the first mile or so of the Sierra
Madre trail as well as several places along Highway 39.

EVENING PRIMROSE FAMILY
Onagraceae

Members of the Evening primrose family are usually herbs,
often with showy flowers borne singly on long stems. The
family is most often found in temperate regions of the New
World. Some of the most interesting flowers on the trail

are members of this family. Evening primroses are unrelated to true primroses, but they probably acquired the name in the early 1600's. When a species was being described, the story is told that the scent reminded the discoverer of the European primroses. He named this family evening primrose and the name stuck.

California fuschia   Pl. 57   *Zauschneria californica*

These flowers have two other rather colorful names: hummingbird's trumpet and California fire chalice. They are also called by their species name of zauschneria. The plants are low and shrubby with many branches. The flowers bloom near the ends of the branches and look like bright red funnels about an inch and a half long. The flowering season is from July to October or later at higher altitudes. Many plants can be found on the Toll Road as well as on the back side of the Sturtevant trail.

Elegant clarkia   Pl. 76   *Clarkia unguiculata*

This flower is indeed elegant. The plants are one to several feet tall, slender, with delicate flowers made up of four diamond shaped petals which grow narrow at the base, widening toward the end. They are a beautiful deep pink color, with orange-red terminals on the stamens. The flowers are frequently found on Upper Winter Creek, Sierra Madre and the Toll Road. They bloom from April to June. You may have to look hard for Elegant clarkia, because it tends to grow back off and on the high side of the trail somewhat in isolation.

Farewell to spring Pl. 66 *Clarkia deflexa*

Although the name implies that spring is over when this flower appears, that's not really the case, since they bloom from early April into July.. The four pink or lavender petals are fan shaped, form a cup, are often flecked with violet. Single plants are frequently found on Upper Winter Creek, Sierra Madre and Toll Road trails. Like many of the plants in these mountains they are named clarkia after William Clark the early nineteenth century explorer of the Lewis and Clark expedition to the Pacific Northwest.

Hooker's evening primrose Pl. 31, 32 *Oenothera hookeri*

The wonderful names of this flower, both the English and Latin, would make it one of my favorites if for nothing else. For starters, Hooker refers to a person, not an occupation. The word *oenothera* connotes that the plant encourages one's taste for wine.

With all of that, "exotic" seems a great term to describe this non-native. Rather large yellow flowers grow on the ends of long stems as much as six feet tall. The plant grows in moist places in semi-shade. The four bright yellow petals form a flower three or more inches in diameter. An interesting characteristic is the cross at the end of the anther. These may grow in Lower Winter Creek or First Water on the Sierra Madre trails, but I've only seen them on Highway 39 at about four thousand feet near a small stream crossing the road. The leaves are long, dark green and lance shaped. It blooms June to October.

Phil's evening primrose   Pl. 33   *Camissonia*

An erect annual found on dry slopes in disturbed or burned areas. Found on the lower reaches of Sierra Madre and Upper Winter Creek trails. The flowers are solitary yellow with four oval petals. Flowers from March to May. I don't know who Phil is.

Sun cups   Pl. 30   *Camissonia bistorta*

A flat lying annual which may be two feet or more across. The four petalled flowers are bright yellow - hence the name - with a brown spot at the base of the petals. Leaves at the base form a rounded cluster; they are quite narrow and one to three inches long. Upper leaves are shorter and wider. The flowers appear in March to June in the open chaparral. Found on Sierra Madre, Toll Road and Upper Winter Creek trails, but not in great profusion.

FIGWORT FAMILY
Scrophulariaceae

A worldwide family with over 3000 species, and well represented in the San Gabriels. Many of the flowers are brilliantly colored, as, for example, the paintbrushes, penstemons and monkey flowers. Many cultivated species are found in local gardens. Characteristically the flowers have five sepals, united, and five bilaterally symmetrical petals, with two lobed upper lips and three lobed lower lips extending from a tubular throat. This family boasts some of the prettiest and most interesting flowers to be found in these parts. The family also embraces one of the widest ranges of coloration in the San Gabriel mountains.

Bush monkey flower   Pl. 45   *Mimulus longiflorus*

This bushy shrub is usually found low to the ground. It secretes a sticky substance, hence the name, but is a lovely plant nevertheless. The flowers vary in color from pale yellow to orange yellow, and bloom profusely. The flowers are jagged edged. If you touch the stigma, its whitish lips may close, sensing that pollen has been deposited. When it realizes you've been fooling it, the flower may then reopen. - but that'll take a while, so don't wait around for it. Flowering is from April to July. The Sierra Madre trail has a number of stands below First Water. Almost at the end of Highway 39 the hillside by the road is a riot of both colors of this kind of monkey flower.

Grinnell's penstemon   Pl. 91   *Penstemon grinnelli*

The delicate color of this low growing flower makes a lovely sight on trailsides at higher elevations. I've most frequently found it near the entrance to Crystal Lake campground on Highway 39, but occasional small patches may be seen high on Sturtevant Falls trail.

The flowers are bilaterally symmetrical, grow no more than a foot off the ground, and are pinkish white to light lavender. You'll find them blooming from March to June. Incidentally, the name is doubtful as in the case of several of these penstemon; grinnelli seems to be the closest. As Shakespeare says, what's in a name? Although the picture doesn't detail the shape of the flower, you should know that it is about an inch long, almost tube shaped, ending in the open mouth shown in the plate with what looks like a hairy tongue coming out of its mouth.

ndian paintbrush   Pl. 61   *Castilleja affinis*

These bright colored beauties are among the most cheerful flowers on the trails.   True red is a rare color among wildflowers, and paintbrush is one of the more common and brightest of the reds.

Few sights are more exciting than to find a stand of ndian paintbrush lining twenty or more feet of the trail, a phenomenon along Upper Winter Creek in several places. Isolated bunches also flourish along Sierra Madre, the Toll Road, Highway 39 and Angeles Crest Highway.   Paint-brush grows to 20 inches high, with bracts (not petals, if you care) extending out several inches from the stem. There are several species on the trails, but the differences are not remarkable.   They bloom from February to May and into June, particularly at higher altitudes.

Keckiella (penstemon)   Pl. 60   *Penstemon cordifolia*

A bushy perennial plant that covers larger shrubs in the chaparral.   Usually found in semi-shaded or protected areas. The bright red tubes have two lobed upper and three lobed lower lips.   The stamens protrude prominently.   You will find many of these penstemon along Highway 39 near the dams on the west side of the road.   Look around the edges of almost any layby.   Incidentally, these wide spots in the sides of the roads mentioned are usually fruitful sites for finding flowers.

Scarlet monkey flower   Pl. 58   *Mimulus cardinalis*

Light green, perennial herb growing to two feet high, generally found in moist areas.   The bright red flowers are about an inch to an inch and a half long.   The plant is not large, but the brilliance of the flower is eye catching. This plant is not often found; actually I've only found one of them only once, and then on Highway 39. The blooming period is from April to October.

Showy penstemon Pl. 89, 90 *Penstemon spectabilis*

This flower really deserves its name. The plant may get three feet high, and be covered from near the base to tip with inch long purple and blue flowers. The flowers are tubes, lighter colored at the base, turning deep blue on the lip opening with two lobes on top, three on the bottom. The Chantry Flat road and Highway 39 are the places most likely to find these spectacular plants, although the upper reaches of Sturtevant Falls has a few. You are likely to find these in bloom from April to June; an especially large patch grows near the Forest Service pine plantings high up Highway 39. Positively passionate colors.

Yellow monkey flower Pl. 44 *Mimulus guttatus*

This annual grows erectly, four inches to two and a half feet high in the chaparral. The flowers are a bright yellow, with a wide throat and upper lobes longer than the lower. Some of the flowers may have bright red dots in the throats, like a case of measles. They are fairly common on the Sierra Madre and Upper Winter Creek trails, less so on the Toll Road. Blooms from April to June. They are easily distinguished from their relative, the sticky monkey flower, because of the smooth edge of their leaves and the more even and yellow brightness of color.

FOUR-O'CLOCK FAMILY
Nyctaginaceae

This family includes the bougainvilleas, the four o'clocks and the verbenas. What appear to be the brightly colored petals are bracts - which probably doesn't matter much to the casual observer. The leaves generally grow opposite one another. The plants may vary considerably in size, from the bougainvilleas gracing many homes in this area, to the foot high verbenas in many gardens.

Mountain four-o'clock   Pl. 69   *Mirabilis californica*

Also called the wishbone bush, this perennial is quite bushy, and in full bloom is almost covered with small pink flowers. The best time to find the flower in bloom is early morning, because the buds open in the evening and close in the morning hours, a very sensible practice in the heat we experience in this area. There are several stands along the Sierra Madre trail at lower levels which flower from March to May. These clumps are easily identifiable because they are quite large, and in flower the pink cast alongside the trail is quite noticeable. Look for them in the first mile after the start of the trail.

GERANIUM FAMILY
Geraniaceae

Taken from the Greek word for crane, geraniums are so named because of the beak like shape of the fruit. The family is world wide, and indeed, the example in this manual was introduced from another continent, although probably very early after the western hemisphere began to be explored. The flowers have five petals, five sepals and five, ten or fifteen stamen.

Crane's bill   Pl. 65   *Erodium cicutarium*

An annual herb, crane's bill is usually found in open areas. The leaves form a rosette close to the ground while the flowers develop on four to twelve inch stems. They are easy to miss because they are less than obtrusive. The seeds are a distinguishing characteristic; they are shaped like a stork's beak, hence the name. Flowers are deep pink, about 1/2 inch across, and bloom January to May. They may be found on Sierra Madre trail, but are more numerous on Highway 39, particularly beyond the East Fork turnoff.

GOURD FAMILY
Cucurbitaceae

These plants are rapidly growing vines, with the five petals of the flowers united at the base. Only two members of the family are found in this area, one of which can be seen on the trails. (See below) Both male and female flowers grow on the same plant, which seems right friendly. They're included here because they are found rather often although they are not among your most attractive flowers.

Wild cucumber   Plate 8   *Marah macrocarpus*

The small white flowers of this trailing vine are easily mistaken for white nightshade, which they resemble in some respects. The flowers have five petals joined at the base each coming to a point, with noticeable stamens (males) or a fat stigma (female) at the center. An early bloomer, cucumber may be found from January to April in sage scrub and chaparral. Roots may grow as large as a hundred pounds, which has given rise to the name of manroot. You will find wild cucumber in the first quarter mile of both the Upper Winter Creek and Sierra Madre trails.

LILY FAMILY
Liliaceae

The lily family embraces more than 1500 species which grow from bulbs or rhizomes. Leaves have parallel veins; petals and sepals are alike in color, except for calochortus (specifically the mariposas.) Many garden flowers are in this group, such as tulips, lilies and iris. This family does not occur with any great frequency on the trails. Indeed, there is only one species pictured in this guidebook because the I have only found this one species of the Lily family along the trails thus far.

Plummer's mariposa lily Pl. 70 *Calochortus plummerae*

One of the loveliest flowers on the trails, and quite unusual, this bulb is also known as pink mariposa. The most distinctive characteristic of the flower is the covering of yellow hairs on the inside base of the petals. They look like the hair inside a cat's ear, although much prettier. The three petals form a flower of about two inches in diameter. The combination of color is quite striking. The long narrow leaves have usually dried up when the flowers bloom, which is from May to July. Mariposa lilies are to be found at some distance from the trail itself along the Sierra Madre trail.

MINT FAMILY
Lamiaceae

Local native members of this large plant family have a number of common characteristics. They are all aromatic; the flowers are two lipped, the upper with two lobes, the bottom with three. The leaves are "opposite"; that is, they grow out of the stem in pairs opposite one another. The family includes many plants we commonly think of as cooking herbs; sage, thyme, mint and marjoram among others. A number of different sages ranging in size from a few inches to feet tall may be found on all the trails and on all the approach roads as well. Some are offensively aromatic when the leaves are crushed; some would make wonderful seasoning for your next poultry dish.

Black sage   Pl. 16   *Salvia mellifera*

The plant is three to five feet tall, with many branches. The leaves grow in pairs opposite one another; are dark green and wrinkled and give off a strong sage odor when crushed. The pale blue white flowers grow in head like clusters all the way around the main stems, two to three inches apart. From April until July this and other members of the mint family may be found on both sides of the Sierra Madre, Upper Winter Creek and Toll Road trails. Several species of sage are quite similar, the main differences being in size and leaf color which may be from dark green to grey.

Chia is one of the most easily distinguished of the mint family on the trails, because the stems look like they are growing right through a thick flower. On closer examination, you'll find that a clump of deep blue but tiny flowers are growing around the stems about every two to three inches, to a height of two feet. The flowers bloom mostly in April and May. Chia seeds may be found in some health food stores where they are sold as a base for a refreshing drink, an herbal tea.

MORNING GLORY FAMILY
Convolvulaceae

The members of this family are generally vines, two of which are found frequently on these trails. The flowers generally have five petals fused into a wide bell shape. Bindweed and wild morning glory are in this family. These two are difficult to distinguish and the differences may indeed be of more importance to a professional naturalist than to a casual hiker. My source books differ as to whether dodder, a parasite, is separate or a member of this family, but it is included here.

Dodder   Pl. 55   *Cuscuta californica*

Dodder is easy to recognize. The plant is leafless, rootless; a parasite which grows in masses on shrubs in the chaparral looking like straw thrown carelessly over the top of its host. The flowers are so small as to be unnoticeable, but the yellow orange vines are unmistakable. Dodder is seen all year round, mainly from April through June.

Morning glory   Pl. 3   *Calystegia macrostegia*

There are two quite similar plants which I have grouped under this heading. One is morning glory and the other is bindweed. The differences are botanical rather than superficially visual. Both are white flowers, growing on long vines, usually close to the ground. The flowers are white, with five fused petals that make them look like a wide mouthed trumpet. Occasionally the back will be ribbed in a light purple, and at other times the flower will appear to have a light green cast. The flowers are about one to one and a half inches in diameter, and bloom from March to August.

MUSTARD FAMILY
Brassiceae (Cruciferae)

These herbs are quite numerous, there being over 3200 species in the northern hemisphere. They are easy to recognize from their four petalled flowers in the form of a cross from which they take their other Latin family name. There are many representatives of the family on the trails, some native, some introduced, several considered "weeds". Cabbage, turnips, radishes and other of our food plants also belong to this group.

Black mustard   Pl. 52   *Brassica nigra*

This prolific annual can be found almost everywhere on any of the trails, except in deep shade. The plant grows two to several feet tall, is rather spindly, and the light yellow flowers are found at the end of long gangly stems. I don't find mustard a terribly attractive plant except where it grows in a mass, which sometimes occurs. Mustard seems to grow everywhere in the grassy areas trailside, usually in scattered thin groups. Blooming season is from March to July. The black in the name is from the color of the seeds.

Honesty   Plate 12   *Lunaria*

Honesty, the flower, is relatively rare on the trails, but may occasionally be found in shady moist places. The four petalled, quite simple, flowers are only about an inch across; the leaves may be a couple of inches long, ovate with pointed tips.The flowers generally grow in flat clusters, even thought the plate shows only a single flower. Look for lunaria along the streams at First Water and the Lower Winter Creek areas, although a couple of my advisors thought I might delete the picture from the book because it is so rare that it is unlikely to be found.

Sweet alyssum   Pl. 22   *Lobularia maritima*

Although not a wildflower, Sweet Alyssum must be mentioned because it is ubiquitous. On all the trails, all year round, the hiker will see this small (six inch tall) plant on trailside blooming some places in isolation, some places in great profusion. The small white flowers grow in clusters at the end of a stalk. Flowers have four petals; leaves are only about one half inch long. Actually, alyssum is a tenacious escapee from domestic cultivation which seems to have made itself quite at home in the wild. Close up to the flower, you can detect a faint sweet odor.

Western wallflower   Pl. 53, 54   *Erysimum capitatum*

The brilliant flowers tend to grow in clumps, often seeming to tumble down canyon walls. These cascades of yellow-orange clusters can be quite spectacular. When in bloom in March to July their strong color is often visible from a considerable distance; for instance, a large mass may be seen from the turnoff to First Water on the Sierra Madre trail blooming at the very bottom of the canyon. The biennial plants are from one to two and a half feet tall, with bunches of flowers on the end of rather stiff stems. Leaves are narrow and from two to five inches long.

NIGHTSHADE FAMILY
Solanaceae

This family is comprised of herbs and shrubs which bear flowers of five united petals. A few species provide foods, such as pepper and tomato, but on the other hand, many are poisonous.

Purple nightshade   Pl. 71   *Solanum xanti*

This lovely little flower with the ominous name is frequently found on the Sierra Madre and Upper Winter Creek trails in the chaparral. The plant grows several feet tall with thin rather unremarkable leaves. The flower is less than an inch across, about the size and shape of a dime. Near the base of each purple leaf is a white spot with a green center. A yellow tip protrudes from the center looking like a tiny corn cob. In bloom from January to May, nightshade may also be found on the entry road to Crystal Lake campground.

Tree tobacco   Pl. 46   *Nicotiana glauca*

Tree tobacco is most often seen as a gangly tree from eight to twelve feet high, with long tubular yellow flowers blooming at the end of long limber branches. The leaves are grayish in color, oval in shape and about an inch and a half long. The flowers may get as much as two inches long, yellow, and may be found nearly all year round. The plant was originally introduced in the late 1800's from South America, and may be found in disturbed areas along virtually all of the trails and approach roads in exposed areas. It is quite poisonous, but the compensation is that it may be found in bloom somewhere, usually along a road, much of the year.

White nightshade   Pl. 13   *Solanum douglasii*

The white nightshade is a somewhat scraggly plant up to five feet high which grows in shady areas of the chaparral stretches of the trails; Sierra Madre, Upper Winter Creek and the Toll Road being the most likely trail locations. The inch long flowers look like five pointed stars with a yellow cone in the center, like the center of the purple nightshade. It blooms practically year round, although so inconspicuously that it is often overlooked.

OXALIS FAMILY
Oxalidaceae

The reason for including a family and species considered by many to be a garden pest is because there is so much of it at the base of the Sierra Madre trail - not to mention in most of the yards near and in the San Gabriel mountains. The plants are perennial herbs, with creeping stems up to a foot long. The flowers are 5 merous; that is, five sepals, five petals, five short stamens, five long stamens and five pistils. The flowering time is March to November. The only species of *Oxalis* included here is found as plate 38. This particular variety has an interesting name, Bermuda buttercup. Those who have found *Oxalis* in their yards know that this is an aggressive, tenacious plant.

PEA FAMILY
Fabaceae (Leguminosae)

The pea family is both large and varied. In the more than 10000 species worldwide are found herbs, shrubs and even trees. As seen in the plates, flowers have five petals, of different sizes and shapes. The top petal is called the banner, the side petals are the "wings" and the bottom petals are joined to form the "keel". The ten stamens and single pistil are enclosed in the keel. Many familiar plants are members of this group, such as peas and beans, peanuts, clover and indigo, the dye. A number of the most attractive flowers found on the trails are species of this family. The species pictured here are among the most interesting and attractive flowers to be found on the trails. Oddly enough, the members of this family found in this area seem to be among the more difficult to identify.

Bush lupine   Pl. 85   *Lupinus longifolius*

The bush lupine is a rather tall, erect shrub, standing as much as five feet high. The flowers appear on long single stalks. Pea shaped, usually a violet color, about 1/2 to 3/4 inch long, some with a yellow spot in the center, they tend to grow on both sides of the stem. A dense planting has been made in the parking lot at Chantry Flat; otherwise they are best found along the Upper Winter Creek trail.

Cassia senna   Pl. 36   *Whoknoesia orcaresii*

I don't know the formal species name of this intrusive Australian found about twenty miles up Highway 39. The flower is interesting because while still in bloom a long pod extrudes from its center. The leaves are like long soft needles; the plant itself is about four feet tall. This intruder is unpopular because it doesn't belong to the local flora and is quite intrusive; nevertheless, the yellow cup like flowers are quite pretty. They bloom from May to July in open areas by the roadside.

Deer vetch   Pl. 49   *Lotus scoparius*

A rather small yellow flower with touches of red which grows on a low, sprawling, somewhat bare stemmed shrub. The oblong leaves are equally small, less than 1/2 inch long. Deer vetch is often found on bare areas, particularly after a fire. A large patch grows just below the point where the Sierra Madre/Winter Creek trails join the Toll Road. Some blooms may be found nearly all year, although the most prolific flowering occurs in the spring. The flowers are found in whorls although they appear to be single blossoms in plate 49.

Large flowered lotus   Pl. 47   *Lotus grandiflorus*

A small shrub 8 to 20 inches high, lotus may be occasionally found in open spots along the Toll Road and Sierra
Madre trails.   The flowers grow in clusters on a single
small stem; they are fairly small despite their name.
Though clearly a lotus, some doubt has been expressed
about whether the flower in plate 47 is indeed the large
flowered species. The leaves are egg shaped, less than an
inch long, and grow alternately on their stems. Flowering
is from February to June. The plant, whatever its name,
will be rather frequently encountered in the chaparral
environment.

Lotus   Pl. 48   *Lotus strigosus*

This annual grows close to the ground, producing small,
typically pea shaped yellow flowers in small clusters. The
stems are somewhat hairy. You will find the plant on the
lower parts of the Toll Road, Sierra Madre and Upper
Winter Creek trails in open chaparral areas. Characteristically, the little plant grows somewhat in the open and
doesn't seem to care for close neighbors.   The flowers
bloom from March to May.

Psoralea   Pl. 79   *Psoralea physodes*

Clearly a leguminoseae, this psoralea will be found only
rarely, and then in shady moist areas. The picture at plate
79 was taken in June at First Water and is the only time
I've encountered this rather unusual plant.

Spanish broom   Pl. 42, 43   *Spartium junceum*

A green stemmed, almost leafless, thickly branched shrub which can get quite tall. Most frequently this plant is found along roadsides such as the approach to Chantry. Some rather large plants may also be found on both Highway 39 (Azusa) and the Angeles Crest Highway (La Canada). When in bloom the bush seems to be covered with a bright yellow fire, a beautiful sight indeed. Individual flowers are the typical pea shape, and grow thickly along the stems from April to June. As I noted about the cover picture in which it appears, Spanish broom is a European import which has become naturalized and is often used to reduce erosion along roadsides. Broom has a tendency to be intrusive and to crowd out less sturdy natives, so it is not a totally unmixed blessing.

Stinging lupine   Pl. 82   *Lupinus hirsutissimus*

A hardy annual generally ten to eighteen inches tall, the plant will be found nestling back off the trail in semi shaded hollows. The stems are covered with nettlelike hairs which can be painful to touch. The flowers grow on single stems in clusters eight or more inches long. The pea shaped flowers are usually deep magenta, shading off to pink, and are among the most attractive and easily recognized on the trails. Found only occasionally on Sierra Madre, they are more prolific on the Upper Winter Creek.

Wild sweet pea   Pl. 15   *Lathyrus laetiflorus*

This climbing vine grows from three to ten feet long and is found twining around shrubs at trailside in chaparral areas. When seen near the edge of the trail the flowers will also be seen cascading down from many feet above, like many other plants shown here. The flowers are light pink to lavender and the banner petal is frequently darkly veined. Flowers are usually less than an inch long, but are noticeable because they grow in groups on a single stem. The pods produced may be three inches long and contain many seeds. Sweet pea is quite common on all the trails at the lower altitudes, and may even be found near the top of the Sturtevant Falls trail within a half mile of Mount Wilson. the vine is less common on the approach roads.

PHLOX FAMILY
Polemoniaceae

This family is mostly North American, and most profuse in the west. Several species are found in this area, three of which are represented here. Phlox are five merous; that is, the flowers have five petals, five sepals and five stamens. Many representatives of the family are found cultivated in gardens around the country.

Eriastrum   Pl. 87   *Idunnoea*

The lovely flowers are quite small and easily missed as you whiz by on Highway 39 near Crystal Lake. The grow in small clumps only a few inches high. The flowers have five petals which are pointed; are a pale blue with bluish purple longitudinal lines. They were found in July at about five thousand feet altitude. They are probably not natives, but don't let that deter you from admiring their beauty. At a distance they appear to be bluer than the picture which was obviously taken very close up and in which they appear more purple in color.

Gilia   Pl. 68   *Gilia splendens*

An annual, this gilia tends to grow in colonies in the chaparral. The flowers are five petalled, pink, on slender stems. Blooms March to May, and maybe later at higher altitudes. The stems are long and scraggly, and the leaves are quite sparse.

Prickly phlox   Pl. 64, 27   *Leptodactylon californicum*

The plant is a bushy shrub which grows to two or three feet in height and bears many flowers. The leave are stiff and sharp pointed. The flowers run an inch to an inch and a half across with a white center which appears to have no stamen. Blooming period is from March to May, and later at higher altitudes. The bushes are frequently encountered on Highway 39 above the East Fork turnoff; I have seldom seen them on the Mount Wilson trails. Plate 27 shows a combination of phlox and chamise in a typically thick and bushy growth of the former.

PINK FAMILY
Caryophyllaceae

Although there are over 2000 species of this family in the Northern Hemisphere, only a few are likely to be encountered on the Mount Wilson trails. Of these, perhaps the most striking is the Indian pink. Flowers usually have five sepals and five petals. The latter may be notched or toothed, giving the appearance of many more petals than there are.

Chickweed   Plate 11   *Stellaria media*

Chickweed is a common annual which grows on trailing stems six to sixteen inches long. The flowers are white, small and grow in leafy clusters. Although there are only five petals, the cleft in each gives the appearance of ten petals. Chickweed blooms from February to September along oak woodlands and in both burned over and cultivated areas beside the trails. A considerable patch may be found near First Water on the Sierra Madre trail. Botanists refer to chickweed as an introduced weed, not even an exotic, but you will find it on the trails nevertheless.

Indian pink   Pl. 56   *Silene laciniata*

The long spindly stems of this perennial may grow as much as four feet tall, with leaves mostly near the base of the plant. The bright red flowers are four petalled with notches or clefts giving the appearance of many petals. Flowers have prominent stamens. The blooming period is from May to July, and the scattered, mostly solitary plants can be found on the Sierra Madre, Toll road and Upper Winter Creek trails. More likely , though, look for them on the roadside along Highway 39. The red is quite eye catching, but the sparseness of the flowers make them difficult to spot easily. The best clump to be found is about half way through the First Water bypass on the Sierra Madre trail.

POPPY FAMILY
Papaveraceae

The poppy family includes both annual and perennial herbs, as well as shrubs. Characteristically the flowers have twice as many petals as sepals and numerous stamens. The petals often appear to have been crushed. The fruit is a capsule. The best known member of the family out here is the California poppy. (See below.)

California poppy   Pl. 35, 36 *Eschscholzia californica*

The California poppy is undoubtedly one of the most popular of all local wildflowers, and familiar to most hikers, but the formal species name is a real killer. (See above.) The solitary flowers have four bright orange petals on stems up to several inches long. The leaves are cut into many narrow segments and are grayish in color. On warm days the flowers roll up to hide from the heat. The Sierra Madre and Toll Road trails as well as Chantry Flat, the Angeles Crest Highway, and Highway 39 all have scattered stands of the plant. Occasionally examples of the flower will be found which are a pale yellow color rather than the usual orange.

prickly poppy   Pl. 1   *Romneya coulteri*

This perennial may grow from three to six feet tall and will be found in colonies in the chaparral. The leaves are gray green, two to six inches long and lightly to deeply indented. The rather large flower has six paper white petals that look as if they had been crushed with a ball of bright yellow-orange stamens in the center. The size and clean color of the white petals and the brightness of the orange center make this a dramatic flower. The plant is sometimes found in gardens because of its strong sweet scent. Prickly poppies bloom May to July and may be found in the chaparral segments of the Sierra Madre and Upper Winter Creek trails as well as along the Chantry Flat road and Highway 39.

Tree poppy   Pl. 34   *Dendromecon rigida*

A perennial shrub as much as ten feet tall with slender dark green leaves one to three inches long. The bright yellow flowers are quite showy; four petals with many stamens. Commonly found on dry hillsides in chaparral. Frequently seen on the approach road to Chantry Flat, the tree poppy flowers from February to June. Once found, the stiff stems of a large plant make it easy to recognize.

PURSLANE FAMILY
Portulacaceae

A family of succulent herbs with only a few representatives on the trails. Only one species is shown, miner's lettuce. Several members of this family are found as ornamentals, and some are edible, as is the species shown here.

Miner's lettuce   Pl. 7   *Claytonia perfoliata*

A low spreading herb which grows about a foot high, miner's lettuce is found in shady places in woodlands, such as on the side of the streams of Lower Winter Creek, Sturtevant Falls and at First Water on Sierra Madre. The small white flowers appear to be growing out of the round smooth edged leaves. The name comes from the fact that the plant is edible and was used as food by early explorers of the region. The explorers must have been very hungry, because miner's lettuce doesn't have much taste.

ROCK-ROSE FAMILY
Cistaceae

Although the family includes both herbs and shrubs, both local examples are shrubs. There are both pink and white flowered species near the parking area at Chantry Flat. Both are introduced (naturalized) rather than native. The plants grow to be about three to four feet high, with flowers of five petals, five sepals, and many stamens. You may notice an aromatic, resinous odor about them.

Crimson spot rock-rose   Pl. 2   *Cistus ladinifera*

This compact evergreen shrub gets three to five feet high, with numerous white flowers about three inches in diameter. The stark white petals look like crinkled tissue paper and have dark crimson, almost black spots at the base. Truly a spectacular flower. Numerous large specimens may be found blooming in March into July close to the parking area at Chantry Flat. They are not natives, having been introduced to this environment in recent years.

Rock-rose   Pl. 67   *Cistus villosus*

The pink rock rose is much like the crimson spot variety, with deep pink, five petalled flowers almost covering the bush. Its petals also resemble crumpled tissue paper. Both rock roses are quite sticky, and exude an aromatic resinous odor, which has been used in perfume and was reputedly the base for the myrrh the magi carried to Bethlehem. Like the crimson spot, several large plants may be found near the Chantry Flat station, particularly along the paved trail descending into the canyon.

ROSE FAMILY
Rosaceae

Family members may be trees, shrubs, vines or herbs. Many common fruit trees belong, such as apples, pears and cherries. The species noted below are frequently encountered on the trails. "A rose by any other name. . .etc."

Blackberry   Pl. 4   *Rubus ursinus*

This native is familiar to almost everyone. We've all seen them, picked and eaten the berries, and been stuck by the thorns. The five petalled white flowers are easily recognized when they are in bloom from March to May. On the trails, blackberry is most frequently found on Lower Winter Creek.

Chamise   Pl. 26, 27   *Adenostoma fasciculatum*

Chamise grows up to fifteen feet high and is a prominent member of the chaparral flora. The white blossoms often carpet the hillsides in the vicinity of the trails. The flowers bloom in large clusters nearly covering these large shrubs. A typical large stand can be seen in plate 100 looking from the Upper Winter Creek trail back toward the Chantry Flat picnic and parking area.

Toyon　　　Pl. 63　　*Heteromeles arbutifolia*

The toyon tree may grow to twenty feet or more in height and is quite a handsome chaparral plant. The long dark green leaves thickly cover the tree, and the berries, which ripen in November and December, grow in bright bunches like holly berries. The flowers are white clusters and may be found in June and July on the Sierra Madre, Toll Road and Upper Winter Creek trails. The berries were eaten by the Indians or used for a drink, yet another herbal tea.

SAXIFRAGE FAMILY
Saxifragaceae

Usually herbs, with small flowers that are radially symmetrical and grow in branched clusters. Only one species is shown here, the Woodland star. Many members of this family are grown as ornamentals.

Woodland star　　Pl. 6　　*Lithophragma affine*

Woodland star is a perennial herb, up to 20 inches high, with few leaves. The flowers have 5 stark white petals and are deeply lobed. Found in shady wooded areas, particularly well out on Upper Winter Creek, all along Lower Winter Creek, and occasionally at First Water on Sierra Madre. Blooms from February into June. This is a charming flower, a little shy, mostly found slightly back off of the trail. The name is well deserved; they look indeed like stars of the woodland.

SPURGE FAMILY
Euphorbiaceae

Although the family consists of almost 8000 species, only one is represented in this handbook. Species in the family include rubber, castor oil, tung oil and tapioca plants. Some are poisonous, some are right tasty (but not castor oil, as I remember.) What appears to be the flower on these plants is in fact a complex of several different types of flowers grouped together to make the whole.

Rattlesnake weed   Pl. 5   *Chamaesyce albomarginata*

A perennial herb which grows flat on the ground, usually making a rough circle about eight to twelve inches in diameter. The dark centered flowers with white margins, from 1/16th to 1/8th inch across in reality are collections of a number of tiny individual flowers. The name comes from the belief that the ground up plant used as a poultice may be an antidote for rattlesnake bite but I wouldn't bet on it.

STICK-LEAF FAMILY
Loasaceae

Most of the 250 species of this family occur in North America. The family consists mostly of herbs with stinging hairs which give the stems and leaves a grayish cast.

ndeed the leaves of the species pictured here have a decidedly grayish tone to them. Only one species of this family is common in the San Gabriel mountain area.

Blazing star   Pl. 28, 29   *Mentzelia laevicaulis*

An easily recognized, large plant with several rather large yellow flowers at the top of sturdy stems. The flowers may be as much as five inches in diameter; they have five slender petals and many long stamens. The long (4 to 12 inches) leaves are narrow with large uneven teeth on the edge. The plant tends to look gray because of the white hairs growing on it. The flowers bloom from June to September, and are particularly prolific along the San Gabriel River East Fork road off Highway 39. The plant produces a dramatic bloom indeed, especially striking where large numbers of the plants cascade down the sides of the cuts along the road. The flowers open toward evening and close early in the day to escape the heat, which seems rights sensible. Evening star is a favorite of mine because it is such a spectacular size, shape and color, and because it has the sense to stay out of the heat.

SUMAC FAMILY
Anacardiaceae

The principal local member of this family is the Sugarbush (see below). The family consists largely of shrubs which grows profusely in the open areas beside the trail on the lower levels. Shrubs commonly reach eight to ten feet or more in height. Poison Oak is also classified in this group, as well as cashews and mangoes. (Some of the former but neither of the latter two, unfortunately, are found on these trails.)

Sugarbush   Pl. 23   *Rhus ovata*

This dense shrub typically grows in the chaparral to as much as 12 feet, although not often that large on these trails.   The leaves are dark, smooth edged and ovate coming to a point at the end. The bushes look like, and do make good ornamentals, because they are handsome and drought resistant to boot.   The flowers grow in tight clusters about three inches in length by two in diameter. Many are visible along the Toll Road, both up and down hill, as well as along the open lower parts of the Sierra Madre trail. The blooming time is from March to May.

SUNFLOWER FAMILY
Asteraceae (Compositae)

The Asteraceae are a large, worldwide family, with about 920 genera and almost 20,000 species. The family embraces herbs, shrubs, vines and a few trees. What appear to be single flowers are in reality a multitude of tiny flowers growing together to look like one.   Actually, the tiny flowers may be one or both of two types. Tube flowers, for example, make up the head of thistles; chicory is made up of ray flowers; and what are easily recognized as sunflowers are groups of both tube and ray flowers. There are many of this family in the area whose differences are small that the yellow and white varieties are frequently referred to as DYCs and DWCs. (See below)

California everlasting   Pl. 19   *Gnaphalium californicum*

This small (foot high) herbaceous plant is easily recognized by the rounded cluster of silvery white flower heads at the top of several leafy stems crowded close together. Isn't this a wonderful name? Indeed, the name is most appropriate because the flowers bloom for a long time, from January into July, and individual plants seem to last a long time. They are usually found a little off the trail back in niches, particularly in the chaparral areas of Sierra Madre and Toll Road. You may also find everlasting near the ranger station at Chantry on both the Upper Winter Creek and the start of The Lower Winter Creek/Sturtevant Falls trails.

California thistle   Pl. 74   *Cirsium californicum*

This biennial is leafy at the base and largely bare on upper parts. The plant may be five feet high, and grows in the open chaparral along the Sierra Madre, Upper Winter Creek and Toll Road trails. It is fairly often seen on Angeles Crest and Highway 39 at lower levels. Blooms appear from April to July with light pink to almost white flat heads about an inch across. The heads consist of a compact bundle of tube flowers.

Cliff aster   Pl. 14   *Malacothrix saxatilis*

Cliff Aster has the good grace to bloom year round, so the flower enthusiast is almost certain to find it no matter what the time of year. The plant is fairly tall with many branches and long narrow leaves. You will likely find it in disturbed areas along the Toll Road or the approach to Chantry Flat. The flower heads are made up of ray florets only, less than two inches in diameter, white, turning light pink as they age. The flower is not what one could call a great favorite of botanists/horticulturists; I suspect because there are a number of hard to identify species and subspecies that are pigeonholed as DWC's - d(arned) white composites.

Common sunflower   Pl. 39   *Helianthus californicus*

At least, that's what I think this plate is. The only one I've ever spotted was on the Sierra Madre trail about a third of a mile up from the beginning of the trail, a rather unlikely spot. This perennial grows up to six feet, with single flowers on the ends of long stems. The plant blooms from March to June in the lower elevations of the chaparral. Unlikely that this is a natural planting, based on the size, variety and location. The smaller sunflower which looks like a many flowered little cousin may be found in the vicinity of the Toll Road, occasionally on the approach to Chantry Flat, and in some profusion on Highway 39.

Dandelion   Pl. 41   *Taraxacum officinale*

You needn't go further than your front yard to find this bright weed, but if you've eradicated it from your property, you will no doubt see the blazing yellow of these Asteraceae on the lower stretches of both the Sierra Madre and Toll Road trails. The flat, multi-rayed heads generally are about an inch across; grow out of a low rosette of lance shaped leaves with backward pointing teeth. The leaves give the plant its name, which comes from dent de lion, French for lion's tooth, a wonderfully fancy name for a garden pest. Young leaves are often used in salads or soup. Dandelion blooms during the winter months into the late spring.

Eupatory   Pl. 18   *Eupatorium adenophorum*

To be completely au courant, you should know the newest name for this species is Ageratina. I like another name for the plant - boneset - because it has reputedly been used medically in connection with setting broken bones. Eupatory is a small shrub growing up to four feet high. Found mostly along the edge of small streams on the trails, such as the on Lower Winter Creek and at First Water on the Sierra Madre trail. Flower heads grow in clusters, and look like small white pin cushions. The leaves are about two inches long, deep green, triangular in shape and saw toothed. The blooms may be found through most of the spring and summer, particularly in areas protected from strong sunlight. Although the shrub has been here for a very long time, botanists classify it as "introduced" rather than native.

Golden yarrow   Pl. 50, 51   *Eriophyllum confertiflorum*

Golden yarrow grows up to eighteen inches high, with many stalks growing out of the base. The flowers grow in clusters, and may best be recognized by their almost wooly appearance. As seen in the plate, they are of an intense mustard color, and make a bright group along open areas of the Toll Road, Upper Winter Creek and Sierra Madre trails. They may be found from January into August.

Leafy daisy   Pl. 75   *Asteraceae radulinus*

The plant is smallish, with many flower heads having irregular light purple ray flowers around the yellowish tube flowers. Leaves are long, lance shaped. Late flowering, July to September, but infrequently found on the trails. The irregularity of the ray flowers is characteristic of the species, but makes it look like someone has been playing "she loves me - she loves me not" and quit in the middle of the game. The family name "asteraceae" is derived from the Latin word for star.

Senecio   Pl. 48   *Senecio*

This member of the sunflower family has so many close relatives that determining it's correct species is a labor of love best left to serious botanists. Suffice it to say that the rather showy bright flower falls in the category of a DYC - d(arned) yellow composite. Naming difficulties aside, this flower and many of its close kin can be found in the chaparral and on the roadsides of the Angeles Crest Highway and Highway 39 in great numbers in midsummer, especially at higher altitudes. As you can see from the plate, the flower seems to be quite attractive to bees.

Thistle   Pl. 73   *Cirsium vulgare*

The national flower of Scotland may be found on all the trails, and particularly on the approach to Chantry Flat. Thistle is recognizable not only by the typical flower shown in the plate, but by the hairy, prickly leaves. The flower is not a single flower at all, but a dense group of tube florets, pink to purple in color. Although not plentiful in total numbers, several species may be found during the blooming season from May to September. Scots probably have found something more elegant to call their particular species of national flower than "vulgare".

Twiggy wreath plant   Pl. 72   *Stephanomeria virgata*

Twiggy is a form of chicory which came to California a rather roundabout way from Holland through Massachusetts many years ago. Long naturalized, chicory is considered an exotic, and goes by several names, among them "wand chicory". The plants are erect, with many branches and long narrow leaves mostly toward the base of the plant. The flower heads are made up of ray florets only (see Asteraceae description above) and are usually white, turning a pale pink/lavender with age. The heads are about the size of a silver dollar. Chicory blooms from April to July, but I've found occasional specimens many other unlikely times of year. This and several other species of chicory are abundant on the Toll Road, Angeles Crest, Highway 39 and Chantry Flat.

White yarrow   Pl. 20   *Achillea millefolium*

Yarrow is a perennial, aromatic herb which grows about two feet high in open spaces in the woods. The white flower heads form dense flat clusters about four inches across. The leaves are long, thin and aromatic and were used by early settlers as a poultice on cuts and bruises. A few plants are to be found around First Water, on the Sturtevant and Lower Winter Creek trails. Yarrow blooms in May and June.

VALERIAN FAMILY
Valerianaceae

The only member of this family included here is the red valerian alias Jupiter's beard. The family itself is not large, and the example found on these trails is a European introduction. The pinkish flowers grow in clusters about the size of a fist on stems of one to two feet high. Red valerian may be found from April to August, principally on the Chantry Flat road; large growths of both red and white valerian may be found in the small park on top of Russian Hill in San Francisco if you happen to be up that way. (Plate 83)

WATERLEAF FAMILY
Hydrophyllaceae

This family includes some of the most enchanting flowers to be found in the San Gabriel mountains. Mostly herbs, flower parts come in fives: five sepals, five petals, five stamens. All the plants shown here are natives.

Baby blue eyes   Pl. 92, 93   *Nemophila menziesii*

What an apt name for such a pretty little flower. The small (3/4 inch) light blue blossoms are found nestling in, under and around grasses, usually in semi shady moist areas near streams. They are particularly abundant near First Water on the Sierra Madre trail, and on the Sturtevant and Lower Winter Creek trails close by the streams, February to June. They are unmistakable and they are quite dear, to use the apt term of one of my advisors.

Caterpillar phacelia   Pl. 86   *Phacelia cicutaria*

Called caterpillar because of the coiled shape of the stems, this phacelia is quite common on the trails. The tiny flowers are white shading to a pale blue, and grow in distinctive coiled clusters. The dark green leaves appear grayish because they are covered with short white hairs. Found on all the trails as well as the approach road and Highway 39. The flowers appear from March to June on plants from one to three feet high.

Parry's phacelia   Pl. 77   *Phacelia parryi*

A fairly small annual, growing from six inches to only a foot and a half tall, this herbaceous annual is frequently found at the edge of the trail on the lower levels of Sierra Madre, Upper Winter Creek and Toll Road. The flowers are bell shaped, deep purple shading to white on the interior, and have five prominent stamens. The color is truly rich. These flowers bear a strong resemblance to the lighter blue Canterbury Bells, which also thrive in this environment. Depending upon altitude, the blooming period may range from March through June. A number of patches of Parry's phacelia are to be found on Highway 39 below the East Fork road. They are also to be found scattered along the first mile or so of the Sierra Madre trail.

Parry's turricula   Pl. 88   *Turricula parryi*

In full bloom this plant is truly magnificent. The shrub itself may be a dense two feet high with long stems extending three or more feet beyond the main plant. Flowers grow in large clusters; and the blue-purple blooms may be as much as two inches in diameter. The leaves may be six inches long, oval and droopy. The last characteristic gives rise to another name for the plant, poodle dog. Turricula is known to cause dermatitis to sensitive skin, so I suggest you not touch the leaves beautiful though the plant may be.

A huge bush grows about a hundred yards up the foot trail to the shooting range on the east side of Highway 39 a few miles beyond the East Fork turnoff. Worth the walk.

Yerba santa   Pl. 21   *Eriodictyon*

This small (two feet high) plant is related to *Turricula*, above, but these flowers are white and grow in smaller clusters. The flowers seem to be a favorite of bees, so be careful around them. They also seem to attract butterflies as shown in the plate. They grow at higher altitudes and bloom during June and July on Highway 39 near Crystal Lake.

THE TRAILS

SIERRA MADRE

The Sierra Madre to Mount Wilson trail is the oldest of all the trails to the summit. Benjamin Wilson, following an old indian footpath, built the trail in 1864 to get timber from the mountain. In 1889 the original Harvard telescope was packed to the top on mule back, piece by piece. About 1890 the original halfway point camp, now called Orchard Camp, was developed into a trail resort, abandoned only in 1940.

This is my favorite trail for a lot of reasons. The environment on the trail is quite varied, from open chaparral to tree shaded, fern covered walks, to deep creek bank forests. It's also the trail closest to my house and easiest for me to get to.

Flowers may be found on the trail at all times of the year; winter, of course, being a bit sparse. Don't expect to see the hillside blanketed with carpets of flowers as you might in other areas. The largest "blanket" I've ever seen was about two square yards of baby blue eyes near First Water. The first mile and a quarter or so is grassy hillside and chaparral and sustains many large flowering shrubs. Among them are ceanothus, sugar bush and tree tobacco. Smaller plants include poppies, lupine, penstemon, various pea plants and occasionally, if you're really lucky, you may find a mariposa lily. Just before the cut off to first water there is a small stand of Indian paintbrush.

The most spectacular display in this area occurs from late April into July, when tall white soldiers of yucca dot the open hillside.

If you think the small white flowers on both sides of the trail look familiar, they should. Sweet alyssum from someone's yard got started here some years back and has aggressively lined the early part of the trail on both sides. Several kinds of sages may also be found in this area, along with related mint family plants like chia. Buckwheat proliferates as does to a lesser extent the California everlasting and its kin.

On a spring hike, just before you go down the cutoff to First Water look down into the canyon for wallflower. You may see stands of this member of the mustard family cascading in profusion down the far side of the canyon.

The environment at First Water is completely different, and so are the flowers. One of the most beautiful is baby blue eyes - isn't that a nice name - which is abundant in the grass along the stream bank. A large shrub with flowers like fuzzy white buttons grows right next to the water in many locations. It is Eupatory - not as nice a name, but an interesting plant nevertheless.

Other plants on the forested stream bank are an occasional Indian pink, larkspur and many woodland stars. From First Water the trail is attractively covered by scrub oak and lined with several kinds of large and small ferns. Wildflowers are not abundant here, because of the lack of light.

Above Orchard Camp a few flowers are to be found here and there to the summit, but not in anything like the variety on the lower parts of the trail.

UPPER & LOWER WINTER CREEK

The hike along the Lower parts of the Upper and Lower Winter Creek Trails is probably the most rewarding of the several possible walks in the vicinity of Mount Wilson. For one thing, there are more different environments in this three or so mile circuit than on any other excursion, which results in a wider variety of flowers. For another, the hike upstream on Lower Winter Creek and down hill on Upper Winter creek is relatively short and easy to traverse.

Start from Chantry Flat at the Ranger station. Before you go down the trail, look around the parking area where plantings of both native and introduced wildflowers have been made. Bush lupine as tall as a man, white and pink rock rose, Spanish broom and several other species have been made into a beautiful array of color. These bloom mostly during the spring, but several varieties bloom at other times of year as well.

Go down the paved fire road to the canyon bottom and turn left where the lower Winter Creek trail is marked. Follow the trail along the creek until you reach Hoegee Camp, about a mile and a half. The trail is in shade most of the way, and in the spring flowers abound.

You will find larkspur, woodland star and carpets of baby blue eyes all along the way to Hoegee Camp. Look for fern, particularly the giant woodwardia growing on the creek bank. Other shade lovers like elegant clarkia and blackberry may also been seen.

When you reach Hoegee Camp, go up the creek on the south side and after a hundred yards or so cross over the ridge to the Upper Winter Creek trail for the return trip. Upper Winter Creek is more open, has more chaparral and therefore has more of the open space loving flowers. Among many others will be found paintbrush, farewell to spring, buckwheat, several varieties of sage, chia and other mints; Parry's phacelia, bush and sticky lupine can be seen from time to time. Virgin's bower vines grow on the chaparral. Purple nightshade and wild cucumber are other smaller flowers to be seen.

Naturally the ubiquitous mustard abounds as do other yellow hued flowers, especially daisy shaped yellows known as DYCs because they are so difficult to differentiate. All in all, you are likely to find more flowers on this jaunt of three miles or so than on any other hike on the Mount Wilson trails.

To go beyond the point of joinder of the lower lengths of these trails, continue to where the Winter Creek trail proper meets the Sierra Madre trail and goes on up to Mount Wilson. The upper reaches of this route have some wonderful vistas, but not much in the way of flowers, at least not in the profusion of the lower levels. Deer vetch, an occasional vine of virgin's bower, a patch or two of lavender penstemon, and now and then a paintbrush are the most likely plants to be encountered.

STURTEVANT FALLS

The lower part of the Sturtevant Falls trail is much the same environment as the Lower Winter Creek trail. The trail starts from Chantry Flat as does the Lower Winter Creek, but instead of turning left at the bottom of the hill, continue up Santa Anita canyon past a number of summer houses, past Sturtevant Falls, a delightful cool locality, and on up the mountain.

Much of this trail traverses coniferous forest in quite deep shade; not a terribly friendly environment for wildflowers, although quite serene and restful.

The lower parts of the trail are home to moisture and shade loving plants, woodland star, larkspur, eupatory, and baby blue eyes being among the most numerous. As on Winter Creek, occasional stands of Woodwardia as well as other ferns may be seen.

At higher altitudes there are stretches of California fuschia which bloom a beautiful scarlet in late fall and early winter. Here and there you will also find an occasional penstemon, usually the light lavender variety.

TOLL ROAD

The toll road has many things to recommend it; there are great views; the slope is more moderate than any of the other trails; the trail itself is quite wide and therefore easy to negotiate. On the other hand, this is the longest of the trails and has less shelter. The trail is better suited to bikers than wildflower seekers, but has its quota of flowers, particularly chaparral flowers. One which blooms in abundance late in the year is the California fuschia. You will find this beauty along the lower parts of the trail in November and December when little else is abloom.

Of course chicory, mustard and many other "disturbed ground" lovers can also be found on this approach to the mountain.

APPROACHES:

Chantry Flat

For those who would like to find flowers but for whom hiking holds no great pleasure, several alternatives are available. One of the most accessible options is the to go up the extension of Santa Anita Drive to the Chantry Flat picnic ground. The station itself displays a profusion of flowers most of the year. On the six mile trip into the canyon many flowers may be found at the right times of year. Stop at any lay-by both to admire the fine views and to look for flowers.

If you walk fifty yards or so up or down from any one of these parking spots you will find numerous species of wildflowers, some of them specific to this highway. In the height of the season I've found as many as ten different varieties blooming within sight of my car. Mustard, tree poppy, tree tobacco, chicory, alyssum (even if it doesn't count as a wildflower), dodder, yucca whipplei, purple nightshade and an occasional penstemon all grow within a few feet of the road.

The showy penstemon are among the most spectacular blooms in these mountains. Finding flowers without going more than twenty yards from your car can be exciting and this highway is a great place to do just that.

Angeles Crest Highway

More distant (at its beginning) from Mount Wilson is the Angeles Crest highway. This trip is worth the effort, for one will probably find more varieties of plants between La Canada and the Mountain top than on the Chantry Flat highway. The environment, especially the altitude, encourages a broader span of growth for one thing; and, of course, the road is simply much longer. The jaunt to Mount Wilson is pleasant in its own right, but wildflower fans will be rewarded by Spanish broom, monkey flower, yucca, several sages, paintbrush and tree tobacco, among others.

Yellow flowers abound at the lower levels in spring. Several species of sages can be found along the middle stretches of the road between La Canada and Red Box. And bright patches of paintbrush flourish on the last stage of the road before Mount Wilson.

Highway 39 (Azusa)

Finally, Highway 39 from Height to Crystal Lake must be included, notwithstanding its distance from Mount Wilson. Several of the pictures in this manual were taken along this road. The climate is roughly the same and these plants probably grow somewhere on the Mount Wilson trails but I simply haven't found some of them on the trails yet.

If you fail to find any of the flowers pictured on the Mount Wilson trails, a trip to Crystal Lake early of a morning in spring may fill the gaps. Besides, the trading post at Crystal Lake campground offers a great breakfast. Another advantage is the Crystal Lake campground; knowledgeable Forest Service staff offer guided nature walks describing and pointing out both flora and fauna of the area.

This road is lavish in the variety, number and size of plants. Among the most prolific are blazing star, heart leaved penstemon, several species of monkey flower and one of my favorites, showy penstemon. Indeed, this area has every reason to be good wildflower territory because the altitude ranges from near sea level to over five thousand feet; and from Azusa to its abrupt termination the road stretches nearly thirty miles.

When in bloom the yucca here make a particularly spectacular display, growing everywhere on the hillsides, up and down the slope, near the road and far away. They offer some great photo opportunities for the camera buff.

Several flowers pictured in this book I've found only on this road, columbine and Hooker's evening primrose among others. For the non hiking wildflower enthusiast, Highway 39 is probably your best bet.